The Cross — the reality of the cross for today

Peter Jeffery

EVANGELICAL PRESS

EVANGELICAL PRESS
Faverdale North Industrial Estate, Darlington, DL3 0PH,
England

Evangelical Press USA
P. O. Box 825, Webster, New York 14580, USA

e-mail: sales@evangelicalpress.org

web: http://www.evangelicalpress.org

First published 2007

British Library Cataloguing in Publication Data available

ISBN 0 85234 642 5   ISBN-13 978 0 85234 642 6

Printed and bound in Great Britain by Biddles Ltd., King's Lynn,
Norfolk

Contents

I. The cross

1. God's plan

The apostle Peter, preaching on the day of Pentecost, explained the cross in terms of both the wickedness of man and the infinite love of God. He accused his hearers very clearly of putting the Son of God to death. Their sin was enormous and they were responsible for it, but overriding this was the plan of God: 'This man was handed over to you by God's set purpose and foreknowledge; and you, with the help of wicked men, put him to death by nailing him to the cross' (Acts 2:23).

The death of Jesus, with regard both to its manner and its purpose, was set and determined by God himself. It wasn't a last minute adjustment to a plan that was going wrong. It always *was* the plan, as the many references and allusions to the cross in the Old Testament make very clear. To the Christian, this is a thrilling truth because it puts our salvation at the heart of God's will and purpose for this world. For the unbeliever, it reveals the folly of rejecting not merely a doctrine, but also the set plan of almighty God. The death of Jesus on the cross was so meticulously planned by God that, over a period of thousands of years, he alludes to it, and shows us it's going to happen — so that when it does at last take place, there should be no doubt as to its meaning. If all this is true, then we had better take it seriously!

Creation

When God created the world, he did so meticulously and carefully, so much so that life on earth would be impossible if things were only slightly different. For example, earth's distance from the sun is exactly positioned to give the earth the correct temperature to sustain human life. If the average temperature of the earth was raised by only two or three degrees, the polar ice sheets would melt, and London would be under twenty feet of water. If our planet were ten per cent smaller or ten per cent larger, human life could not exist. In the same way, the 23.5 degree tilt of the earth axis is not some arbitrary thing, but necessary for life.

Such meticulous work was needed by God to sustain human life on earth. In the same way, God was equally painstaking when he planned our salvation. God's way is the only way of salvation, and we cannot amend it without fatal consequences. Man is now discovering that his own foolishness and greed may be affecting the earth's atmosphere and contributing to global warming and climate change. We are all aware of the danger to life if that global warming trend continues and the polar ice caps keep melting.

We cannot play around with God's meticulous plans either in creation or in salvation. We need the cross exactly as God planned it. There can be no variation, no amendments — and no changes. The cross is God's set purpose and we must accept it as such.

In the garden of Gethsemane, the disciples, not understanding what was taking place, tried to prevent the arrest of Jesus by meeting force with force. Jesus stopped them with the warning, 'But how then would the Scriptures be fulfilled that say it must happen this way?' (Matt. 26:54). Then he made this statement concerning his coming death: 'But this has all taken place that the writings of the prophets might be fulfilled.' Over and over again, the New Testament repeats the same truths, not merely in regard to the general idea of the Saviour's death, but even to specific details such as the betrayal (compare Acts 1:16 with Zechariah 11:12-13).

Why did God do it?

There are two reasons why God planned our salvation as he did. The first is that he wanted to, and he wanted to because he loved us. The other reason is that God did it because he had to if we were to be saved. Without a Saviour, all sinners will perish eternally. Both reasons are found in John 3:16: 'For God so loved the world that he gave his one and only Son, that whoever believes in him shall not perish but have eternal life.' In other words, it's God's love that makes the cross possible, and it's God's holiness that makes it necessary.

That God is love is a precious truth that is accepted by practically everyone, but the meaning we give to love is not always biblical. Modern man confuses love with sentimentality, and sees God's love as a sort of general benevolence which has no other purpose but our happiness. It then follows that God will not punish sin. Consequently, every notion of hell is dismissed as incompatible with the idea of a 'God of love'. Such thinking is seriously flawed because, although it's true that God is love, this is not the only thing that's true about God. He is also holy. The love of God as seen on the cross saves sinners, but from what are they saved? The Bible has only one answer to that: sinners are saved from perishing, from the consequence of their sin, from the wrath and judgement of God upon that sin. In John 3:16, why are people perishing? Because God is holy and will not, and cannot, tolerate sin. In 1 John 4:9-10, we see both the love and holiness of God linked together: 'This is how God showed his love among us; he sent his one and only Son into the world that we might live through him. This is love; not that we loved God, but that he loved us and sent his Son as an atoning sacrifice for our sins.' Why was it necessary for Jesus to be an atoning sacrifice or propitiation for our sins? Because God in his holiness had declared that the wages of sin was death. He will not wink at human sin or pretend that it is nothing. Sin has to be dealt with in accordance with his own law.

The atoning sacrifice, or propitiation, that Jesus made on the cross satisfies the law of God and thus satisfies God's holiness. The word 'propitiation' means that, on the cross, bearing our sin and guilt, Jesus faced the wrath of God instead of us, and fully paid on our behalf the debt we owed to the broken law of God. At Calvary, Christ made it possible for a holy God to be propitious — or favourably inclined — towards us, even though we sinners had broken his holy law. At Calvary, Christ's suffering was sufficient to cover the sins of all his chosen people throughout all of history. God dealt with the problem of sin in the only way that could satisfy his holy justice and enable him to move in and break the power of Satan in sinners' lives. The fact is that it's the holiness of God that dictates the events on Calvary. In his love, God decided to save sinners from the consequence of their sin, but it's God's holiness that dictates exactly how this is done. A way of salvation had to be found that in no way contradicts the character of God. This means that sin must be punished and not just glossed over.

The only way

Sin is essentially a rejection of the character and being of God. It refuses God's way and is an insult to his holiness. It's a hatred of all God stands for. But no person can live in this world apart from the ways of God. God has made us in such a way that we need oxygen to live. If a man puts his head in a plastic bag, he will die because there will be no oxygen for him to breathe. There's plenty of oxygen all around him but, by his action, he has chosen to cut himself off from God's provision for life. He deliberately ignores God's way and the consequences are terrible.

In much the same way, God has made a provision for our salvation. If a sinner is to be saved, he or she needs love, grace and mercy, and these flow in abundance from the Lord Jesus Christ. The gospel is not a complicated message understandable only by theologians. The gospel simply says, 'You are a sinner and Jesus is God's one and only provision for your salvation; believe the gospel; repent of your sin; have faith only in Jesus and live.' But many will not do this. They ignore the meticulously planned way of God and put their heads in a plastic bag called morality, good works or religion. God's way is the only way. It also is a sure way. God planned a perfect and foolproof way of salvation. God's way can save the young and the old, the clever and the dull, the rich and poor. No one is barred from this way because of race or colour. This way is through the Lord Jesus Christ, and it is called the gospel.

II. The cross in the Old Testament

2. Isaiah 53

In the book of Isaiah, there are four passages which are known as the Servant Songs: Isaiah 42:1-9; 49:1-13; 50:4-11 and 52:13 – 53:12. On several occasions, the New Testament quotes these passages to describe the ministry of Jesus. For instance, Acts 8 quotes Isaiah 53 and Matthew 12:17-21 quotes Isaiah 42. Isaiah was writing in about 700 B.C., so how could he so accurately describe Jesus? There can only be one answer and it's that God was revealing these truths to the prophet. In chapter 53, Isaiah presents to us a remarkable description of our Saviour's death. When the Ethiopian eunuch in Acts 8 was reading this portion of Scripture, he could not understand it, but his ignorance was dispelled when 'Philip began with that very passage of Scripture and told him the good news about Jesus' (Acts 8:35).

Description of the Saviour

Other parts of the Old Testament describe Jesus as the 'Lily of the Valley', the 'Rose of Sharon', 'outstanding among ten thousand and altogether lovely'. These descriptions are, in fact, the exact opposite of Isaiah 53:2-3: 'He had no beauty or majesty to attract us to him, nothing in his appearance that we should desire him. He was despised and rejected by men, a man of sorrows and familiar with suffering. Like one from whom men hide their faces he was despised, and we esteemed him not.' In Isaiah 53, we do not see Jesus as the Son of God in all his unique glory and majesty, but as man's sin-bearer dying on the cross in agony and shame. Isaiah doesn't paint a pretty picture, but it is the same Jesus whom Solomon describes as 'altogether lovely'.

Isaiah had already described Jesus as 'Emmanuel, God with us'. What we then see in Isaiah 53 is what God came into this world to do. It's staggering and almost unbelievable, but certainly true. In verse 2, we see the humble beginning of his life. He grew up on the streets of Nazareth and no one paid any special attention to him. He was like an insignificant root in dry ground; a piece of vegetation that seemed doomed to wither away, so he scarcely was noticed. King Saul, the first king of Israel, stood head and shoulders above other men, and there-fore could not help but be noticed. King David had a very attractive physical appearance so that eyes would have been drawn to him. The Jesus of Isaiah 53 wasn't like that. In spite of this, there was a beauty and loveli-ness about his character, and one could expect that this would attract some. But it was not so. We see in Isaiah 53 the complete and absolute humiliation of Jesus. This was Emmanuel, God become man.

What happened to him?

The whole picture in Isaiah 53 is one of suffering. In his life, Jesus had been familiar with suffering. In spite of

this, there was a beauty and loveliness about his character. In his death, the suffering reached untold depths. The
words the prophet uses to describe what Jesus had to
endure are significant: stricken, smitten, afflicted, pierced,
crushed, punished, wounded, oppressed. That's a
frightening list. Worst of all, Jesus did nothing to deserve
it. He was God's righteous servant (v. 11) who did no
violence nor spoke any deceit (v. 9). We might expect,
therefore, that he would plead his innocence and demand justice, but no: 'He did not open his mouth; he
was led like a lamb to the slaughter' (v. 7).

Why did it happen?

The answer to this question is most extraordinary. It's so
staggering that most people refuse to believe it. They say
it's impossible and even immoral. Yet Isaiah states the
answer very clearly and gets an abundance of support
from the rest of Scripture. It happened because it was
God's will. Jesus was stricken by God (v. 4), and 'It was
the Lord's will to crush him and cause him to suffer'
(v. 10). This brings us back to Acts 2:23 and the truth
that the death of Jesus was in accord with God's set
purpose. Christ's death and how he died were all part of
God's plan. The plan is unfolded in Isaiah 53, and no
fewer than ten times we are strongly told that Jesus died
for us, instead of us.

   Jesus was suffering not for any wrong he had done but
on behalf of the guilty. That is why there was no objec-
tion from him. To say that Jesus died in the place of
sinners is not enough. The Bible will not leave it there

and insists upon using key words like 'propitiation' and 'blood' to describe what Jesus was doing on the cross. Isaiah 53 goes further. The atoning death of Jesus is shown to be one of humiliation. It wasn't a quiet, dignified death, but the sinless Jesus was identified with the wicked (v. 9) and transgressors (v. 12). He is killed with criminals as if he is no better than they.

More than that, he is *crushed* (v. 5) by the law and justice of God. In verse 5, the Authorized Version and the Revised Authorized Version use the word 'bruise', but that's too weak a word to describe what was happening. A bruise is uncomfortable and leaves a mark, but crushing is agonizing and destroys. The Hebrew word is *daka* and is used of people being trampled to death. This was the death of Jesus.

The reason for all this is summed up in verse 10: 'The Lord makes his life a guilt offering.' This is the language of the Old Testament sacrificial system and simply means that if a sinful man, under the wrath of God, would approach God, he must first sacrifice a spotless, innocent victim in his place. This did two things: it showed that the man acknowledged his sin and that he came trusting in God's way to make atonement for that sin.

The wonder of the gospel is that God now makes himself an offering for our sin. He sacrifices not some animal, but his own Son: Jesus, the Lamb of God who takes away our sin. Once we see that, Isaiah 53 becomes clear. We are all guilty and under God's wrath, but because he loves us, God lays our sin and guilt upon Jesus and pours out his judgement upon our substitute, our sin-bearer. Jesus is the guilt offering for our sin. It's the punishment of our Saviour that brings us peace

(v. 5). The Bible says that there's no peace for the wicked, and this is so because of our sin. On the cross, Jesus deals with sin, and this brings us peace.

The song begins in Isaiah 52:13 on a note of praise and victory and ends on the same note at the end of chapter 53. The cross is a great success story. Because of his death, Jesus now has an offspring — the people whose sin he has borne. He sees this offspring (v. 10), and he is satisfied that he has totally fulfilled all that God the Father wanted him to do. He has justified many (v. 11) and made the guilty acceptable to God. This was his purpose in coming into the world, and that task is now finished. When Philip explained this to the Ethiopian in Acts 8, that man's life was transformed, and he 'went on his way rejoicing' (Acts 8:39). This is the experience of all believers: Our joy and peace rests only upon what Christ has done for us. It can be your experience when you turn to God in repentance and faith.

3. Zechariah

Zechariah, along with Haggai and Malachi, was one of a trio of prophets the Lord sent to the remnant of his people who returned to Jerusalem after the Babylonian captivity. These were days of great spiritual weakness, and the people were in a low condition. Zechariah's ministry was therefore meant to encourage them. The prophet does this in the greatest possible way. He points them to the mercy and grace of God in the coming Messiah, the Christ. In fourteen fantastic Old Testament chapters, consisting of a series of visions, the New Testament gospel is set before us four hundred years before Jesus was born.

The great perplexing question for any sinner who feels the weight and burden of his/her sin is: 'How could I ever be acceptable to a Holy God?' Zechariah 3 shows us that the answer is in being clothed with the perfect righteousness of Jesus. There can be no gospel without the doctrine of imputed righteousness, and in this vivid picture of the priest in filthy clothes, the prophet shows us God's answer to the yearning of our heart. Christ himself is introduced in verse 8 as 'my servant, the Branch', and the great gospel promise is that God 'will remove the sin of this land in a single day' (v. 9).

In Zechariah 6:12-13, there's a lovely portrayal of Jesus as priest and king. David Baron says of these verses: 'This is one of the most remarkable and precious

Messianic prophecies, and there's no plainer prophetic utterance in the whole Old Testament as to the Person of the promised Redeemer, the offices he was to fill, and the mission he was to accomplish.'[1]

The Palm Sunday entry of Jesus into Jerusalem is shown in Zechariah 9:9 and quoted by both Matthew and John. The betrayal of Jesus by Judas is foreseen in amazing detail in chapter 11:12-13. All this reminds us that there wasn't anything vague about God's plan of salvation. Nothing takes God by surprise because he planned it. In chapter 13, two truths stand out, both essential for our salvation and both reassuring for guilty sinners: The fountain and the sword speak of the grace and justice of God working for us.

The fountain

The Lord has opened a fountain to deal with sin and impurity. This fountain of grace and mercy makes life-giving water available to guilty sinners. The idea of God being a fountain of grace to his people didn't originate with Zechariah. In Psalm 36:9, David says of God, 'For with you is the fountain of life; in your light we see light.' The Lord complains through Jeremiah of the people forsaking this fountain: 'My people have committed two sins: They have forsaken me, the spring of living water, and have dug their own cisterns, broken cisterns that cannot hold water' (Jer. 2:13).

The fountain is a vivid illustration of the fullness and never-ceasing mercy and love of God. Zechariah 13:2-6 reveals the emptiness of formal, man-centred religion. In contrast to this pathetic charade, the fountain really does cleanse from sin and impurity. Here's something that works.

Today people are despairing at the blatant and arrogant march of evil. Crime of all sorts abounds, and the largest groups of criminals are teenagers. People are asking the politicians to 'do something', but the politicians are as useless as the false prophets of verses 2-6. The only answer is God's fountain of grace and love. To open this fountain cost God an infinite price because the fountain is the blood of his Son. The proof of this is to be seen in verse 7: '"Awake, O sword, against my shepherd, against the man who is close to me!" declares the Lord Almighty. "Strike the shepherd, and the sheep will be scattered, and I will turn my hand against the little ones."' There's no doubt that this text refers to the cross, because Jesus quoted it in Matthew 26:31-32 a few hours before Calvary and applied it to his death.

The sword

In verse 7, it's the Lord himself who is speaking, and he is not talking to any person, but to the sword. In Scripture, the 'sword' is a symbol of judicial power. The sword which is the instrument of violent death is also the symbol of justice, so in Romans 13:4 a ruler is called the one who bears the sword. The Lord is calling upon the sword of judicial power not to defend, but to strike God's own shepherd. This shepherd is 'the man who is close to me', or as another translation puts it, 'the one who is my companion' or 'kinsman'. C. F. Keil writes, 'God would not apply this epithet to any godly or ungodly man whom he might have appointed shepherd over a nation. The idea of nearest one (or fellow) involves not only similarity in vocation, but continuity of physical or spiritual descent, according to which he whom God calls his neighbour cannot be a mere man, but can only be One who participates in the divine nature, or is essentially divine.'[2] Specifically, the shepherd is Jesus, God's one and only Son.

Almighty God calls the sword of judgement to smite his Son. The teaching here is clear — the death of Jesus was a judicial act. Jesus endured the just and proper penalty of God's law upon sin which is death. It was the sheep which had sinned, not the shepherd, and it was therefore the sheep who deserved the sword's blow. But the shepherd interposed himself and offered his own heart to the sword. The shepherd bears the sheep's sin upon the cross and dies in their place. It's God who instigates this; God planned the cross. God laid on Jesus our sin. God made Jesus to be sin for us. God delivered Jesus up for our sin. God opened the fountain. Sin is such a vile and terrible thing that nothing less than the death of a holy and sinless substitute could free us from its grip. The Son of God was the only one qualified to die for sinners. The dam of divine wrath broke upon Jesus our sin-bearer at Calvary, and the fountain of grace was opened.

The last words of chapter 13 are thrilling for any believer. It's because of both the fountain and the sword that we are able to call upon the name of the Lord with confidence. God answers that call with the most reassuring of all words: 'They are my people.' And it's only on the basis of God owning us as his that we are able to say, 'The Lord is our God.'

4. The Day of Atonement

God's way of salvation did not start in the New Testament when Jesus came into the world. From time to time in the Old Testament the Lord designed certain events to be pictures of what Jesus was going to do when he came. For instance, the Day of Atonement is clearly expounded in Hebrews chapters 9 and 10 in terms of the death of our Saviour.

Approaching God

Verse 1 of Leviticus 16 reveals what a serious business it is for sinners to approach the holy God. Aaron's sons, Nadab and Abihu, were priests, but that did not mean they could approach God in worship in any way they liked. We are told in Leviticus 10:1 that 'They offered unauthorized fire before the Lord contrary to his command.' What exactly this involved we do not know, but it was contrary to God's prescribed way and they died because of it. So God warns Aaron in Leviticus 16:2 that he is not to come into the Most Holy Place whenever he chooses or he too will die.

The Most Holy Place, or Holy of Holies, was the small room in the Tent of Meeting, or tabernacle, where the Ark of the Covenant was kept. The lid of the ark was called the mercy seat, and, in this small room, God's presence was deemed to be known in a special way. Therefore it was not to be entered lightly. Only the high priest was allowed in, and then only once a year on the Day of Atonement. If the mercy seat was approached in God's prescribed way then there was great blessing for the people, but if it was approached in any other way, it meant death.

All this may sound very strange to us today! But this symbolizes two very important truths that are just as relevant now as they were in the days when Leviticus was written — namely, the unutterable holiness of God and the exceeding sinfulness of man. God wants us to come to him, but our sin is an insurmountable problem that must be dealt with first. The Old Testament system of sacrifices was instigated by God to remind man that his sin was a barrier. The sacrifice of bulls and goats and lambs was a symbolic way of cleansing the sinner that had one essential common factor: 'Without the shedding of blood there is no forgiveness' (Heb. 9:22). The blood of animals could not really deal with sin but served to remind the people of the *fact* of sin (Heb. 10:3-4).

Two goats

Several things took place on the Day of Atonement, but let us concentrate on the two goats mentioned in Leviticus 16:7-11. One goat was killed and its blood was taken by the high priest into the Most Holy Place and sprinkled on the mercy seat. This symbolized the turning away of the wrath of God from man's guilt. Mercy, instead of judgement, came to the sinner.

The other goat, called the scapegoat, was brought to the high priest, who laid his hands on the animal's head and confessed the sins of the people. Symbolically the sins were transferred to the scapegoat, and the goat, when sent into the desert, took away the sins of the people (vv. 20-22).

All this was symbolic. These things were, says Hebrews 9:1, 'external regulations applying until the time of the new order'. That new order came with the Lord Jesus Christ. What was symbolic on the Day of Atonement became reality in Christ. The death of our Saviour is the only sacrifice that God now recognizes. When Jesus died on the cross, he accomplished what the two goats symbolized: he turned away the wrath of God from us and he took away our sin. Christ's sacrifice was once for all (Heb. 10:10).

When people approach God today, the only way that is acceptable to the holy God is through the Lord Jesus Christ. We must know that he has dealt once and for all with our sin; only then can we come with confidence into the presence of God.

5. The Passover

God was determined to set his people free from the slavery of Egypt. Repeatedly he had sent to Egypt's ruler the message, 'Let my people go' (Exod. 10:3). Pharaoh refused to obey even after God had sent nine terrible plagues to Egypt. The Lord had been patient with this hard-hearted Egyptian, but 'Now the Lord said to Moses, "I will bring one more plague on Pharaoh and on Egypt. After that, he will let you go from here"' (Exod. 11:1). The tenth plague was that on a given night the angel of death would be sent by the Lord to kill the first-born son in every home in Egypt.

When this terrible event took place, God would protect his own people. The Lord would make 'a distinction between Egypt and Israel' (Exod. 11:7), but this would not happen automatically. To benefit from this provision of the grace of God, the Israelites had to do as God commanded them in Exodus 12:3-11.

The blood

The blood of the sacrificial lamb sprinkled on the door-frames of the Israelite homes was crucial for their deliverance. God said, 'The blood will be a sign for you on the houses where you are; and when I see the blood, I will pass over you. No destructive plague will touch you when I strike Egypt' (Exod. 12:13).

The first-born in the Israelite homes were spared from the judgement of God that night, not because they were Israelites, but because they were sheltering under the blood of the Passover lamb. The distinction that God put between these two peoples was not a national, or cultural, or even religious one. The distinction was of obedience to the revealed purpose and grace of God. The difference between the Egyptians and the Israelites that brought salvation was the blood on the doorframes, for God had promised, 'When I see the blood, I will pass over you.'

Christ our Passover Lamb

The significance of the Old Testament Passover for us today is revealed in many New Testament references — none more so than 1 Corinthians 5:7, where Paul states that 'Christ, our Passover Lamb, has been sacrificed.' The apostle is saying that the Old Testament event was meant by God to be a picture for us of the meaning of the death of Christ. Jesus is the Lamb of God who shed his blood to deliver us from sin. The apostle Peter tells us clearly that we are redeemed 'with the precious blood of Christ, a lamb without blemish or defect' (1 Peter 1:18-19).

The original Passover delivered the Israelites from the judgement of God and set them free to enjoy new life. They were no longer slaves but free men and women enjoying the provisions and mercy of the Lord. So for us

today the death of Christ our Passover Lamb delivers us
from the guilt and penalty of our sin. In Christ we have
new life and can now enjoy all that God has promised
his people.

If you are to become a Christian, it must be by the way
that God has laid down. The Lord God does not say,
'When I see your kindness and generosity and religious
observances then I will pass over you in judgement and
pardon all your sin.' God's way of salvation is through
the blood of Christ, through his atoning death on the
cross. For us today the equivalent of sheltering under the
blood of the Passover lamb is to trust alone in the death
of the Lord Jesus Christ to make us acceptable to God.
When we do that, God's judgement passes over us, and
our sin and guilt are fully pardoned.

6. Psalm 22

Psalm 22 was written by David about a thousand years before Christ was born, yet it is more than merely a description of David's experience. It is prophecy and it also describes what is going to happen to the Messiah. 'Messiah' is a Hebrew word meaning 'anointed one'. The Greek equivalent is the word 'Christ'. Jesus Christ is the Messiah, and he suffered, years after the psalmist wrote the words, all that is described in Psalm 22. Compare the first verse of the psalm with Matthew 27:46; then compare verses 7 and 8 with Matthew 27:41-44 and Psalm 22:18 with Matthew 27:35.

Forsaken by God (vv. 1-5)

Jesus did not merely quote these words on the cross; he experienced them. The testimony of God's people down the centuries is to the absolute faithfulness of God. Psalm 22:4 is the normal experience of God's people — they trust in the Lord and he helps them. David said in Psalm 37 that he had never seen the righteous forsaken. There was no one more righteous than Jesus but he was forsaken by God. So why was Christ forsaken by God the Father?

The explanation is to be found in verse 3: God is the Holy One. We have already seen something of the holiness of God, and if we ever forget this we shall be in danger of failing to understand the true character of God and why he acts as he does.

The holy God laid our sin and guilt upon his Son, and Jesus our substitute bore it alone. On the cross he was facing the wrath and judgement of God upon our sin. That is why the Father turned his back on him. The Bible says that God is so holy that he is of purer eyes than to behold evil and cannot look on iniquity. So when Christ bore our sin he was left to tread the winepress of divine wrath alone. There was no angel to help him, no friend to comfort him, no Holy Spirit to assure him, no smile of a heavenly Father to encourage him. Christ hung alone on the cross with our sins, facing hell and all the hatred of the world, and — far worse — facing the holy judgement of the Lord upon the sin of his people.

The loneliness and agony of the cross (vv. 6-21)

Jesus is the Lord of glory, the express image of God, yet in verse 6 he describes himself as a worm and not even a man. It is sin — our sin — that has done this.

In verses 7 and 8 we see this sin erupt into hatred and scorn of Jesus. Verses 14-17 show us the physical agony of the cross. This is the cost of salvation. This is what sin does. At the cross we see man's hatred of God, but we also see God's hatred of sin as the Holy One deals with the sinner's substitute. Sin is an insult to the holiness of

God. It separates man from God and leaves man with no hope in the world.

Deliverance (w. 22-31)

In the final verses of the psalm, Calvary is past, and now we see something of Christ's triumph. The lament of verse 1 turns into the joyful assurance of verse 24: 'He has not hidden his face from him but has listened to his cry for help.' The forsaking was very real, but it also was only temporary, and now sweet communion is once again enjoyed with the heavenly Father. Sin has been dealt with, divine justice is satisfied, and now divine love breaks out in the praise of verse 22 and the worship of verse 29. And note especially the last glorious proclamation of verses 30 and 31. 'Future generations will be told' — told what? They will be told what Jesus has done on the cross; told of God's love and grace and mercy and provision of salvation; told of Jesus dying in our place.

You have been told the same thing all the way through this book. What do you intend to do about it? Follow the advice of verse 26 and seek the Lord. Seek him for forgiveness and pardon for all your sin. Seek him for love and grace to save you.

7. The curse of the law

We have seen already that man's greatest problem is his sin and guilt before the holy God. Sin is a problem because it puts us under the curse of the law. The curse of the law is its rightful punishment upon all those who break the law of God. We have all broken that law; therefore we are all under this curse, and without deliverance from it there can be no salvation. We cannot at the same time be under the curse of the law and also be acceptable to God. So what is the answer?

Paul gives us the answer in one word: Christ. Christ is the answer because Christ is God's answer. Man's answer is always law — that is, his own efforts. But this does not work. It is our inability to keep God's holy law that is our problem. In Galatians 3:10, Paul quotes from Deuteronomy 27:26 and spells out the problem: 'All who rely on observing the law are under a curse, for it is written, "Cursed is everyone who does not continue to do everything written in the book of the law."'

We are under this curse if we do not continue — that is, *all* the time — to do *everything* the law requires — that is, there is to be no failure at all. The law allows for no failure: it must be total obedience every moment of our lives, otherwise we are deemed to be guilty. By that standard of perfection we have no hope.

Our only hope is the grace and mercy of God. Because God loved us, he sent the Lord Jesus Christ into the world to redeem us from the curse of the law.

Christ became a curse

The statement in Galatians 3:13 that Christ became a curse for us is one of the most amazing in the Bible. Immediately we are brought into the realm of a doctrine that the Bible teaches over and over again — namely, the substitutionary death of Christ for his people. The fact that Paul speaks of Christ becoming a curse reminds us that, unlike us, Christ was not under the curse of the law. Jesus was sinless, so it was not possible in a normal situation for him to be under this curse. But when God laid on him our sin and guilt, the consequence was that the Son of God became a curse. It was 'for us'. Jesus became responsible for our sin and therefore our curse was put upon him.

The tree

Paul further explains this by quoting again from Deuteronomy: 'Cursed is everyone who is hung on a tree' (Deut. 21:23). This Old Testament verse is not directly referring to crucifixion, because that means of execution was not known when Moses wrote Deuteronomy. The verse refers to the taking of the dead body of an executed criminal and nailing it to a tree. This was deemed to be a most terrible thing, a symbol of divine rejection.

A tree is not a cross, but nevertheless on five occasions the New Testament writers speak of the cross as a tree (Gal. 3:13; 1 Peter 2:24; Acts 5:30; Acts 10:39; Acts 13:29). They do this to link the death of Jesus with Deuteronomy 21:23. They are emphasizing the truth that on the cross Christ became a curse for us. He paid the penalty of our violation of God's law. By his death he redeems us from the curse.

Faith

Galatians 3:14 tells us why Christ redeemed us: 'in order that the blessing given to Abraham might come to the Gentiles through Christ Jesus, so that by faith we might receive the promise of the Spirit'. The greatest blessing given to Abraham was to hear God saying, 'I will be your God and you will belong to me.' It was the blessing of belonging to God and this becomes ours in salvation.

The way to obtain this blessing, says Galatians 3:14, is by faith: not our own efforts, not our goodness, not our morality or religion, but faith in what Christ did for us on the cross. Faith is not a way of achieving salvation; it is the God-appointed way of receiving the gift of salvation. Faith is not a step in the dark: it is the exact opposite; it is a step out of the dark into the light of Christ. Faith looks to Jesus alone. It has stopped trying to save itself, and it casts itself upon the grace and love of God in Christ for full and free salvation.

Do you have this faith? Because of who Jesus is and what he has done for us, trusting Jesus is a most reasonable act. Stop trying to save yourself and turn to Christ, who is God's answer to your problem of sin.

III. The cross in the New Testament

8. Gethsemane — prophecy becomes reality

Immediately to the east of Jerusalem lies the deep Kidron Valley, which separates the city from the Mount of Olives. Late on the Thursday night before Passover, after leaving the upper room and the remarkable events of the Last Supper, Jesus, with the eleven apostles, crossed the valley to the garden of Gethsemane. There in that quiet place, more remarkable events took place that set the scene for the first Good Friday. What took place there, apart from Calvary itself, is surely the most awful and solemn happening recorded in Scripture. Here we are shown the most private and intimate feelings of Jesus as he prepared himself to face the cross in a few hours time.

The Bible is full of prophecies about the death of Christ. God pulls no punches as he describes in terrible detail in such passages as Psalm 22 and Isaiah 53 the events that were to take place. But Gethsemane is not prophecy; it is the fulfilment of God's plan. Jesus in the garden is not in heaven inspiring David and Isaiah to write these prophetic words; he is in Gethsemane, and the cross is only a short distance away on the other side of the city. Charles Spurgeon said of Gethsemane: 'Here we come to the Holy of Holies of our Lord's life on earth. This is a mystery like that which Moses saw when the bush burned with fire and was not consumed. No man can rightly expound such a passage as this; it is a subject for prayerful, heart-broken meditation, more than for human language. May the Holy Spirit graciously reveal to us all that we can be permitted to see of the King beneath the olive trees in the garden of Gethsemane!'[1]

The hour had come, and the awful reality of the cost required to purchase our salvation is made evident. Jesus had always known what was required, but now, in Gethsemane, he begins to feel it. Gethsemane is very much about feelings, about deep emotions. Jesus says, 'My soul is overwhelmed with sorrow to the point of death' (Matt. 26:38). Luke tells us that the intensity of Jesus' emotions was such that he sweat drops of blood (Luke 22:44). Mark says that Jesus began to be deeply distressed and troubled (Mark 14:34). Hugh Martin writes, 'These expressions are far from conveying the great force and emphasis of the original.'[2] Martin goes on to say, 'Here we have the grief of him who is the ever-blessed God; the sorrow and weakness and fear and trembling of him who is the Lord God Omnipotent; the tears, prostrate agonies and cries of one who is now seated on the right hand of the Majesty in the heavens, angels and principalities and powers being made subject to him!'[3]

It was no easy thing that Christ was going to do for his people. Dying is one thing, but dying a substitutionary, atoning death is something quite unique — and only the Lord Jesus Christ ever had to experience that. The cost of salvation is as immense as the love of God is deep, and both of these are seen in Gethsemane.

Why was Jesus in Gethsemane?

Jesus went to Gethsemane to pray (Matt. 26:36). It was a quiet place, and Jesus often went there with his disciples (John 18:1-2). Prayer to Jesus was like breathing — it was the most natural of activities. But this time there were vital reasons to pray. He was about to face such experiences as no one had ever known. The events of Calvary were monumental. They were such that even Jesus was in deep distress at the prospect of them, and his only relief was prayer. Prayer is not an escape from problems, but a facing up to difficulties in the presence of God with an acceptance of his will.

Before going to Gethsemane, Jesus spoke to his disciples about the experiences that he was to face. He said in John 14:30, 'The prince of this world is coming.' Calvary was to be the great battleground of eternity. Satan and all his hosts were ready to do their utmost to foil Jesus in his mission of salvation. What a scene must have been in the mind of Jesus when he uttered these words. He saw the prince of darkness assembling his legions of hate and evil, and all were set in array to hurl themselves at the Son of God.

Frightening though that prospect was, there was something even more terrible that was to happen at Calvary. Jesus knew that after Gethsemane he would not be able to call upon heaven to help him because God was about to smite him. God would lay on Jesus the sin of his people, and all of heaven's wrath against sin would fall upon him as our sin-bearer. Both heaven and hell would be pounding Jesus. All this was about to break upon him, so he needed to pray. God did not let him down

and sent an angel to strengthen him (Luke 22:43).
Remember that Jesus was the incarnate God. He said
that all power in heaven and earth was given to him.
That this was no idle boast was seen in his ability to raise
the dead, heal the sick, calm the storm and walk on
water. Jesus is the omnipotent God. How then can an
angel strengthen the omnipotent one?

Two natures

Jesus is the God-Man. Probably the greatest mystery of
all is that in Jesus there existed two natures. They were
both real and both equal — one did not detract from the
other. Before Bethlehem, Jesus was in heaven with God,
and he was God. His divine nature knew nothing of the
frailty and temptation of human nature. At Bethlehem, at
his birth, God became man. This was emphasized by
Isaiah's prophecy that they would call the newborn babe
Emmanuel, which means 'God with us'. The divine
nature took to itself human nature. This wasn't a blend-
ing of two natures; it wasn't a mixture of the human and
divine. Jesus is not part God and part man. He is both
fully God and fully man, as much God in the manger as
when he created the world.

Both the deity of Christ and his humanity are essential
for our salvation, but as Louis Berkhof said, 'Men have
sometimes forgotten the human Christ in their reverence
for the divine. It is very important to maintain the reality
and integrity of the humanity of Jesus by admitting his
human development and human limitations. The splen-

dour of his deity should not be stressed to the extent of obscuring his real humanity.'[4]

It was because Jesus was man that he could die and could feel the anguish of all that was involved in his atoning death. He needed strengthening, and in Gethsemane, God the Father sent an angel to do that. Jesus needed it because he was feeling as never before the terrible cost of salvation. The writer to the Hebrews tells us that, 'During the days of Jesus' life on earth, he offered up prayers and petitions with loud cries and tears to the one who could save him from death' (Heb. 5:7). He felt things in Gethsemane that he had never felt in heaven. He began to feel the weight of human sin that was to be laid upon him and the weight of divine justice that would also come. So he prayed with loud cries and tears. One of the old writers, Robert Traill, wrote, 'He filled the silent night with his crying, and watered the cold earth with his tears, more precious than the dew of Hermon, or any moisture, next unto his own blood, that ever fell on God's earth since the creation.'[5]

Did the angels reassure Jesus that this was God's will, and that there was no other way? Did the angel also remind Christ that the cross wasn't the end, but that resurrection would follow? In his humanity, Jesus needed to know from heaven that, although for a few hours he would be forsaken by God, not for one minute would he cease to be loved by the Father.

But the man Jesus needed something else also. He needed the support and comfort of his apostles. When he went to the garden to pray he didn't go alone. He took the apostles with him not as a matter of courtesy but because he needed them. This was particularly true of Peter, James and John. He said to them 'Stay here and keep watch with me' (Matt. 26:38). But they failed him. We can see his obvious disappointment when he found them asleep, 'Could you men not keep watch with me for one hour?' (Matt. 26:40).

These three, who had experienced the glories of the transfiguration, could not share in the agonies of Gethsemane. They slept while Jesus agonized. The Saviour was being driven more and more into isolation. A year previous, most of his disciples had left him (John 6). Soon the apostles would do the same thing, and the most terrible of all desertions would come when the Father would forsake him. In Gethsemane, the tidal wave of God's wrath because of our sin is beginning to build up.

'Like a flint'

In the third of Isaiah's four Servant Songs (Isa. 50:4-11), the prophet sees the Messiah setting his face 'like a flint' to go to the suffering that the Lord had set for him. He is determined to be totally obedient to the will of his Father. In Gethsemane, despite the intensity of his sorrow, Jesus wasn't seeking to avoid the cross. In fact, going to this particular garden was making the cross inevitable. We read in John 18:2-3, 'Now Judas, who betrayed him, knew the place, because Jesus had often met there with his disciples. So Judas came to the grove, guiding a detachment of soldiers and some officials from the chief priests and Pharisees.' Judas knew Gethsemane as a favourite spot of Jesus and was able to lead the soldiers there to arrest him.

Commenting on this passage, D. A. Carson writes: 'The time (at night) and location (away from the city itself, removed from crowds that could become mobs) provided the betrayer with an ideal venue in which to bring the arresting officers right up to Jesus. Having sanctified himself for the sacrificial death immediately ahead, Jesus doesn't seek to escape his opponents by changing his habits. Instead, he goes to the place where Judas Iscariot could count on finding him.'[6] Commenting further on the words in John 18:4, Carson goes on to say: 'Jesus, *knowing* all that was going to happen to him...' (emphasis added)[7]

All four gospels present Jesus as *knowing* what would happen. For example, in the Synoptic gospels (Matthew, Mark and Luke), the passion predictions, the agonizing prayer in Gethsemane and the calm insistence that he could call on legions of angels for help are otherwise meaningless. But the theme is especially strong in John's gospel: Jesus offers up his life in obedience to his Father, not as a pathetic martyr buffeted by the ill winds of a cruel fate. Jesus went willingly and obediently to the cross, but he went feeling deeply the cost involved in purchasing our salvation.

9. Gethsemane — Christ's deep sorrow

There's sorrow, and then there's *sorrow*. Some people are perpetually sorrowful and rarely smile. Their personality and nature tend automatically to pessimism. When you see such people in sorrow it's so usual to their normal state that you pay little attention to it. Others are of a much different temperament. They are always smiling and happy, so when they are sorrowful, it's so unusual that you have to ask, 'Why?'

Neither of these two extremes was true of Jesus. He was the most perfectly balanced person there has ever been. When Scripture describes him as the Man of Sorrows, it's not referring to his temperament, but to something very special that was to happen to him. It's true that we are never told in Scripture of Jesus smiling or laughing, but to draw major conclusions from that as to his temperament would be wrong. Jesus was the most normal man it was possible to be; he knew both joy and sorrow. But the sorrow of Gethsemane had little to do with temperament.

The intensity of Jesus' experience in Gethsemane was such that Luke says he sweat drops of blood. The night was cold enough for the soldiers to light a fire in the courtyard, yet Jesus sweat drops of blood. Mark says that the sorrow was such that Jesus was deeply distressed and troubled. This was not the sorrow Jesus experienced at Lazarus' death when he wept. Gethsemane was so different that even the Son of God was amazed at its intensity.

What caused such sorrow? J. C. Ryle said, 'I believe the agony in the garden to be a knot that nothing can untie but the old doctrine of our sin being really imputed to Christ, and Christ being made sin and a curse for us.'[1] Ryle is correct and fully in accord with the teaching of Isaiah 53. Why was Jesus a 'man of sorrows'? Because, says the next verse in that remarkable chapter, he carried our sorrows. He did that because the Lord had laid on him the sin of us all. But in Gethsemane this had not yet happened. Jesus at that time wasn't bearing our sin; he wasn't yet facing the wrath of God instead of us; he had not yet become a curse for us. The sorrows of Gethsemane arose from the prospect and thought of the sorrows of Calvary.

The cup

Twice, in Matthew 26:39 and 26:42, Jesus refers to what he is about to experience as 'the cup', and it was the prospect of drinking from this cup that caused Jesus such deep sorrow. The sorrow wasn't caused by the thought of having to face death. Death wasn't the problem to Jesus that it is to us. Jesus described death as having restored to him the glory that he had with the Father from before creation. 'The cup' refers to what was involved in the death.

In the Old Testament, the idiomatic use of 'drinking the cup' refers predominantly to God's punishment of human sin, as the following verses make clear: 'Awake, awake! Rise up, O Jerusalem, you who have drunk from the hand of the Lord the cup of his wrath, you who have drained to its dregs the goblet that makes men stagger' (Isa. 51:17). 'This is what the Lord, the God of Israel, said to me! Take from my hand this cup filled with the wine of my wrath and make all the nations to whom I send you drink. When they drink it, they will stagger and go mad because of the sword I will send among them' (Jer. 25:15-16). Jesus had always known that one day this cup of God's wrath would be put into his hand. But now in Gethsemane the concept is soon to become a reality, and he feels something of the dread of drinking that cup.

Made sin

On the cross God laid on Jesus all the sin and all the guilt of his people. We can sometimes say this rather glibly without much thought or understanding as to how it felt for Jesus. How would you feel if you were made responsible for someone else's sin? And if that responsibility involved blame and resulted in punishment, how would you feel then? Yet the fact is that there's no sin that someone else may commit that all of us are not capable of committing. Sin is so much the dominant factor in our nature and behaviour that we are actually capable of committing *any* wrongdoing. But Jesus is the God-Man, sinless and perfect. Not only that, but he detested all sin: 'Your eyes are too pure to look on evil; you cannot tolerate wrong' (Hab. 1:13).

It was this Holy One who was made sin. When Jesus bore our sin and died, it wasn't theoretical, but very real. It had to be real if the law of God was to be fully satisfied — a violated law would not accept a theoretical atonement. So when we say that Jesus was 'made sin', what sort of sin did he bear? Paul in 1 Corinthians 6:9-11 reveals for us something of the burden that Jesus bore for his people: 'Do you not know that the wicked will not inherit the kingdom of God? Do not be deceived; neither the sexually immoral nor idolaters nor adulterers nor male prostitutes nor homosexual offenders nor thieves nor the greedy, nor drunkards nor slanderers nor swindlers will inherit the kingdom of God. And that is what some of you were. But you were washed, you were sanctified, you were justified in the name of the Lord Jesus Christ and by the Spirit of our God.'

Hugh Martin writes, 'True, the sins which were charged upon him were not his own, but they were so laid upon him and so became his, that he could not merely endure, but accept as righteous, the penalty which they entailed... And if the punishment of these sins was thus not in semblance, but in reality accepted by Jesus as justly visited upon himself, must it not have been because the sins themselves had first been made his — verily, really his — to every effect save that alone of impairing his unspotted personal holiness and perfection? And if they were his to bring him wrath unto the uttermost in their penalty, must they not have been his to cause him grief and sorrow inconceivable in their imputation? True, they were not personally his own; and so they were not his to bring self-accusation, self-contempt, despondency, remorse, despair. But they were his sufficiently to induce upon his holy soul a shame, humiliation, sorrow — yea, sore amazement — as he stood at his Father's tribunal, accountable for more [sin] than child of man can ever account for unto eternity.'[2]

Sin separates

The second implication of Jesus bearing our sin is that if sin separates us from God, then it also separates our sin-bearer from God. Jesus knew this was going to happen. Therefore, when on the cross he cried out, 'My God, my God, why have you forsaken me?', he was not merely quoting Psalm 22, but was actually experiencing that awful separation. Jesus was to drink this cup of God's wrath to the very dregs. So fully did Jesus make himself one with sinful man that he entered into the God-forsakenness that is the lot of all sinners: He died their death.

All this, and much more, was in the cup of God's wrath, and Jesus had to drink it all. There were no short cuts: this was the only way if men and women were to be saved from the guilt and consequence of their sin. The Old Testament Day of Atonement pictures for us what was taking place on the cross.

In Leviticus 16, the Day of Atonement is described for us. In verses 7-10, we are told of two goats: one was killed and its blood was taken by the high priest into the Most Holy Place and sprinkled on the mercy seat, symbolizing the turning away of God's wrath from man's guilt. Mercy, instead of judgement, came to the sinner. The other goat, called the 'scapegoat', was brought to the high priest, who laid his hands on the animal's head and confessed the sin of the people. Symbolically the sins were transferred to the scapegoat, and the goat, when sent into the desert, took away the sin of the people (vv. 20-22). All these things were symbolic. They were, says Hebrews 9:10, 'external regulations applying until the time of the new order'. That new order came

with the Lord Jesus Christ. What was symbolic on the
Day of Atonement becomes reality in Christ. The death
of our Saviour is the only sacrifice that God now recognizes. When Jesus died on the cross, he did what the two
goats symbolized — he turned away the wrath of God
from us and he took away our sin. It was the prospect of
all this that caused our Saviour such sorrow in Gethsemane. The Lord Jesus drained the cup.

Because of this, the Christian will never have to face
this sorrow. We will never have to face the wrath and
condemnation of God.

10. Gethsemane — God's will

There are two things uppermost in the mind of Jesus in Gethsemane. One is the awful prospect of being the sin-bearer for his people. The other is the determination that God's will should be done. The deep sorrow that's overwhelming his soul is not the dominant force guiding the actions of our Saviour. The sorrow is not warping what had always been his greatest concern, namely, to do the will of his Father. He comes in prayer with his face to the ground in a spirit of reverence and awe. He is not demanding or pleading. The words, 'if it is possible', are not to be interpreted as Jesus groping for a way out. He is merely making a request, but the request is couched in an acceptance that what really matters is the Father's will.

Neither is there any reluctance in the prayer. 'We do not enter at all into the mind of Christ if we limit his language to a mere expression of his willingness to drink that cup which could not pass from him. We must understand the Saviour as intensely desiring that the will of God should be done',[1] says Hugh Martin. If, then, Jesus is willing to accept God's will, why does he ask, 'If it is possible, may this cup be taken from me'? He asks because the cost of God's will being done was immense to Jesus. The thought of what was involved prompts Jesus to ask if there's not another way. He knows the answer is no, and he is perfectly willing to accept this, but it's putting him under enormous pressure. The sorrow was great in Gethsemane because of the great agonies he knew were awaiting him at Calvary.

What was God's will?

Jesus was not in disagreement with God's will — far from it! He is one with the Father in all things and, therefore, fully in accord with what God planned to do. On the cross, in the death of his Son, God was going to deal with human sin.

There wasn't anything new about God dealing with sin. In Genesis 3, he dealt immediately with the sin of Adam and Eve. Their sin was exposed, judgement was pronounced, and they were driven from God's presence. In Genesis 4, Cain was left in no doubt what God felt about him killing his brother: 'My punishment is more than I can bear', he said. Then in Genesis 6:5-7, 'The Lord saw how great man's wickedness on the earth had become, and that every inclination of the thoughts of his heart was only evil all the time. The Lord was grieved that he had made man on the earth, and his heart was filled with pain. So the Lord said, "I will wipe mankind, whom I have created, from the face of the earth — men and animals, and creatures that move along the ground, and birds of the air — for I am grieved that I have made them."'

And so it was, right through the history of God's people. Israel in the wilderness knew God's dealing with their sin, and so, too, did David after his adultery with Bathsheba. Sin pained and grieved the heart of God, but, in one sense, those dealings in the Old Testament cost God nothing. He was punishing sinners, but he wasn't atoning for the sin, nor providing eternal salvation for the guilty ones.

It is true that God instituted a sacrificial system which symbolized atonement and salvation, but this system couldn't really deal with sin. It was 'an illustration for the present time, indicating that the gifts and sacrifices being offered were not able to clear the conscience of the worshipper. They were only a matter of food and drink and various ceremonial washings — external regulations applying until the time of the new order' (Heb. 9:9-10). Additionally, we read: 'The law is only a shadow of the good things that are coming — not the realities themselves. For this reason it can never, by the same sacrifices repeated endlessly year after year, make perfect those who draw near to worship. If it could, would they not have stopped being offered? For the worshippers would have been cleansed once for all, and would no longer have felt guilty for their sins. But those sacrifices are an annual reminder of sins, because it is impossible for the blood of bulls and goats to take away sins' (Heb. 10:1-4).

These laws and pronouncements involved little or no direct cost to God himself. God was deeply grieved by the sin of the people, but the remedy cost man, not God. Demands were made for people to make atonement. God gave the instructions, but man had to provide the sacrifice. The dealing with sin at the cross was different. This cost God. Indeed, it touched the very being and person of God. At the cross, God is not now merely making demands; he himself is providing the sacrifice and making the atonement. The sacrifice would be Jesus — and the atonement would be made through the shedding of Jesus' blood.

Now we face a seemingly impossible dilemma: At Calvary, God is not merely going to deal with sin by punishing it. He is going to provide full salvation for guilty sinners. But how can God do both these things? Sin must be punished. There can be no God-given salvation at the expense of justice — and the legal and just punishment for sin is the death of the sinner. So it would seem that justice leaves no room for salvation; they seem to be mutually exclusive: How can God be just — that is, deal with our sin as his law demands and as our sin deserves — and at the same time offer guilty sinners salvation? That's the dilemma.

Substitution

The biblical answer to this seemingly impossible dilemma is the doctrine of the substitutionary death of Jesus. Leon Morris says, 'The richness of New Testament teaching on this subject centres on Christ. Was there a price to be paid? He paid it. Was there a victory to be won? He won it. Was there a penalty to be borne? He bore it. Was there a judgement to be faced? He faced it. View man's plight how you will, the witness of the New Testament is that Christ has come where man ought to be and has met in full all the demands that might be made on man.'[2]

The teaching on substitution in both Old and New Testaments is vast and varied. In the Old Testament, we have indications of this truth often in the historical narratives. For instance, when Abraham was called upon to sacrifice his son Isaac in Genesis 22, God intervened and provided a ram to die instead of Isaac. It's seen more clearly in the death of the Passover Lamb in Exodus 12, and perhaps even more so in the details of the Day of Atonement in Leviticus 16. The great Messianic Song of Isaiah 53 tells us no fewer than ten times that Christ died for his people: he was pierced for our transgressions; he was crushed for our iniquities; the Lord has laid on him the iniquity of us all.

In the New Testament, the teaching is direct and clear: 'God made him who had no sin to be sin for us, so that in him we might become the righteousness of God' (2 Cor. 5:21). Moreover, 'He himself bore our sins on the tree, so that we might die to sin and live for righteousness; by his wounds you have been healed' (1 Peter 2:24), and: 'For Christ died for sins once for all, the righteous for the unrighteous, to bring you to God' (1 Peter 3:18).

This was God's plan to deal with human sin. It was no theoretical arrangement, but was very real and very costly. It touched the heart of God because it cost him the death of his Son. And for Jesus the cost was beyond imagination. God imputes or credits our sins to him, and he as our substitute becomes responsible for them. As our sin-bearer, he pays in full the punishment those sins deserve and faces the wrath and judgement of God. The awful reality of all this is heard on the cross when Jesus cries out, 'My God, my God, why have you forsaken me?' He was experiencing what the writer of Psalm 22 could only imagine.

We need to grasp the significance of this. He who hung on the cross had been for all eternity the object of God's love. And during the thirty-three years Jesus had been in this world, he had enjoyed unbroken communion with God the Father. What then must it have meant for him to be forsaken by God? The hiding of the Father's face was for Jesus the most bitter ingredient of the cup God had given him to drink.

No wonder he cries out in Gethsemane, 'If it is possible, may this cup be taken from me.' It would only have been possible if God were willing to give up his plan to save guilty sinners, if God were prepared to scrap the plan made in eternity and prophesied in Scripture. Was this a dilemma for God? Would he forsake Jesus, his holy Son, or forsake us guilty sinners? As Christians, we can be eternally grateful that it was God who faced this dilemma and not anyone else. Anyone else would have understandably rejected us. But it was no dilemma for God. His love for us was so amazing and so wondrous that he forsook his own Son in order to save us.

Some people have great trouble accepting this truth of substitution, even regarding the idea as immoral. Leon Morris answers them: 'To put it bluntly and plainly, if Christ is not my substitute I still occupy the place of a condemned sinner. If my sins and my guilt are not transferred to him, if he did not take them upon himself, then surely they remain with me. If he did not deal with my sins, I must face their consequences. If my penalty was not borne by him, it still hangs over me. There is no other possibility. To say that substitution is immoral is to say that redemption is impossible.'[3]

It was God's will that sin should be punished, and the idea of an innocent substitute dying instead of guilty men and women was his. He doesn't expect us to provide an innocent substitute from among our friends — and, anyway, there are no innocents, for all of us have sinned. God demands a substitute and he, himself, provides the substitute. God gives the only sinless Man to die for us.

11. Calvary

The word 'Calvary' is a very special one for Christians. This was the place where Jesus died for them and purchased their redemption. The hymn writers delight in using the word, but, surprisingly, it's only found in the Bible once — in Luke 23:33 in the Authorized Version (AV): 'And when they were come to the place, which is called Calvary, there they crucified him.' In many modern translations, the word is not found at all. The place is usually called 'the Skull' or 'Golgotha'. All the versions are correct; the difference is that they take the name from different languages. The Aramaic word is *golgotha*. 'Calvary' is the Latin translation of the Greek word *kranion*. Both the Latin and Greek words are translations of the Aramaic word which means 'skull'. So probably the most accurate English translation would be 'the Skull'. But whatever name we use, it's the events that took place there that make the place special.

From Gethsemane to Calvary, Jesus says very little. It wasn't a time for talking but for suffering. The sufferings of our Saviour, physically, mentally and spiritually, were terrible, but, strangely, the Old Testament tells us more of these than the New Testament. In the four Gospels, the writers continually focus our attention not just upon Jesus, but also on the people around the cross — Pilate, Herod, Caiaphas, the Pharisees and so on. We are shown their part in the crucifixion and their attitude towards Jesus so that we may honestly examine ourselves before the cross of the Lord Jesus Christ.

The onlookers

Luke tells us about the crowd and their leaders (Luke 23:35). The rulers sneered, scorned and made fun of Jesus. They made it abundantly clear what they thought and where they stood — they were against Jesus. The people, however, were more restrained; they stood watching. This was a public execution and it was a holiday time, so they came to watch. They were not bitterly and fanatically opposed to Jesus like their leaders; they just looked, curious but rather indifferent.

Here were two seemingly different responses to the cross, but in God's sight there was no difference. Open opposition or mere indifference to the crucified Jesus — both are sinful reactions and stem from hearts dominated by sin. The person who is an arrogant atheist and delights in mocking and abusing the name of Jesus, and the one who would not dream of doing such a thing but is not committed to Jesus and just stands watching, (sometimes curious, sometimes indifferent, sometimes in church, sometimes not) are both the same in God's sight.

The 'if' of doubt

As you go through the events that surround Calvary, you see that what links the various groups is the 'if' of doubt. The rulers said, '*if* he is the Christ' (Luke 23:35); the soldiers, '*if* you are the king of the Jews' (v. 37); the thief in verse 39 voices the same doubt: 'Aren't you the Christ?' None of these believed that Jesus was God's Christ. They were spiritually blind: that's what makes a person either opposed to or indifferent to Jesus. Both reactions stem from the same root of unbelief.

Jesus says in verse 34 that they don't know what they are doing, and Paul says in 1 Corinthians 2:8 that if they had known, they would not have crucified the Lord of glory. Does this ignorance excuse them or render them innocent? No, it does not, because they *should* have known. Plenty of evidence had been given them and they unintentionally acknowledged this when they said, 'He saved others' (v. 35). This ignorance reveals the deadly grip sin has on human nature. It blinds minds, deadens souls and enslaves the will and conscience. They didn't know but they were still responsible.

Sin acts on us all the way that alcohol acts upon a drunken man — he doesn't know what he's doing. If he drives a car and kills someone, he may truthfully be able to say, 'I can't remember anything about it.' But the law will still hold him responsible. And when a man dead in sin breaks the law of God, the Lord holds him fully responsible and demands that the penalty be paid. This is the terrible situation of all sinners, and it's a hopeless situation apart from the grace of God. It was because he

loves us and sees our hopelessness that God sent his Son
to deal with our sin and guilt.

Grace at work

There was one man at Calvary who realized who Jesus
was; on that awful day he was able to rejoice with joy
unspeakable. The penitent thief was an amazing miracle
of grace. Even as the sky darkened and God forsook his
Son, at that very moment the angels of heaven were rejoicing over one sinner who repented.

In the story of the two thieves, we can see God's sov-
ereign grace in saving sinners. Both were physically near
to Christ, both saw and heard everything, both were
criminals who deserved judgement, both were dying
men, both were sinners who needed forgiveness — yet
one died in his sin and the other was saved. A fact like
that ought to teach us humility. As Christians, we are no
better than anyone else. The difference between the
saved and the lost is the grace of God. It should also
teach us a sense of urgency. It has been said of the two
thieves that one was saved at the last moment of his life
so that no one might despair, but only one so that no
one might presume. Sinners need to be saved, and they
need to be saved *now*.

The work of grace in the redeemed thief follows the
same path as it does in all the people of God. The steps
of repentance vary little no matter what the sinner's
background or circumstances. There are four:

1) Fear of God (Luke 23:40). Proverbs says that the
fear of God is 'the beginning of wisdom' and, we might

add, it's also the beginning of salvation. It's a realization that we are answerable to a holy God who will not tolerate sin; one who has said that no one who sins will enter his presence. It's the awareness that God means what he says and that he is not to be trifled with. Jesus said, 'Do not be afraid of those who kill the body but cannot kill the soul. Rather, be afraid of the One who can destroy both soul and body in hell' (Matt. 10:28). The fear of God is the beginning of an awareness of the reality and presence of God, and of a true respect for him. There's no salvation without this.

2) Confession of sin (v. 41). Fear leads to confession. When we see God, we also see ourselves for what we are. We stop trying to justify ourselves and realize that our sin deserves hell. This conviction of sin will, in the grace of God, cause us to look for a Saviour.

3) Recognition of Jesus (v. 41). 'This man has done nothing wrong', said the thief. In other words, Jesus is not like us. We are sinners; he is sinless. We are humans; he is the Lord, the Son of God. He is our only hope and the only one who can save us. There are no 'ifs' of doubt here, just a quiet confidence in the ability of Jesus to deal with sin.

4) Prayer for mercy (v. 42). This man was a criminal and therefore crucified by the Roman authorities. He was a sinner and therefore condemned by God. His situation was hopeless and he deserved nothing good. But he rested on divine grace and asked simply that Jesus would remember him. It's beautifully simple — to some it may seem too simple — but to be remembered by Jesus is enough. Christ's answer to this man epitomizes both his power and willingness to save sinners. The man was

saved at the hour of the Saviour's greatest weakness as he hung on the cross, forsaken by his Father. Surely, this is power! The thief was saved as a guilty sinner at the point of death with nothing in his past life to recommend him, and nothing in his present position except a prayer of repentance. In the morning he was a condemned criminal; in the afternoon he was a redeemed sinner, and by the evening he was a glorified saint.

12. The moment Jesus died

Several remarkable physical phenomena took place when Jesus was crucified. If any single one of these happened today it would make the front page of most newspapers. But at Calvary all three happened almost at the same time. There was a total darkness from 12 noon until 3:00 p.m.; an earthquake occurred; and many dead people were raised to life. All these are recorded in Matthew 27:45-53. The people who were in Jerusalem and experienced these things must have wondered what was happening. Few probably realized that this was the activity of God. But we are told that at least one man realized these events were connected to the death of Jesus. The Roman centurion in charge of the crucifixion said, 'Surely he was the Son of God.'

There was a fourth event that was nothing like as dramatic as the other three but was of far more spiritual significance to those who want to know the way to God: 'At that moment the curtain of the temple was torn in two from top to bottom' (Matt. 27:51). In the middle of recording the events of the death of Jesus, Matthew, Mark and Luke suddenly break off their reports to mention a curtain being torn about half a mile from Calvary. It seemed so insignificant and out of place but clearly it was of great significance to the three Gospel writers.

Matthew says, 'at that moment', meaning that this curtain was torn at the exact moment Jesus died.

Matthew, Mark and Luke saw this as the clearest sign as to the meaning of the events taking place on the cross. To them it signified that the way to God was being opened up and that God himself was pulling down the barriers he had imposed.

History of the temple curtain

The veil was originally part of the Old Testament tabernacle, which was a sort of portable church that the people of Israel, the Jews, carried with them during their wilderness wanderings. God himself had designed the tabernacle, and he had given very detailed instructions to Moses as to how it was to be built (Exod. 25-31).

In the tabernacle there were two rooms, the Holy Place and the Most Holy Place. The Most Holy Place contained only one thing — the Ark of the Covenant with its lid of solid gold, which was called the mercy seat. A curtain separated the Holy Place from the Most Holy Place (Exod. 26:31-33). The curtain or veil was woven in strands of purple, blue and scarlet onto a white linen background and measured 15 feet by 13.5 feet (4.5 metres by 4 metres). The significance of the curtain was that no one was allowed past it into the Most Holy Place except the High Priest, and even he was allowed to pass only once a year on the Day of Atonement, carrying the blood of the sacrificial animal that was to be sprinkled on the mercy seat to appease the wrath of God. The curtain barred the way to the Most Holy Place where God was deemed to dwell.

When the wilderness wandering ended and the Israelites settled in the Promised Land, eventually King Solomon built a great temple patterned on the tabernacle. This included the Holy Place and the Most Holy Place, separated by the curtain, and was governed by exactly the same laws concerning the High Priest and the Day of Atonement. By the time of Jesus, Solomon's temple was gone, but Herod's temple had replaced it, again with the curtain keeping people out of the Most Holy Place.

The curtain said, in effect, 'Keep out.' It barred everyone, except the High Priest once a year, from the mercy seat and from the presence of God. Worship and sacrifice took place all around the temple, but the curtain barred the people from the essential presence of God. Then, at the exact moment when Jesus died, the curtain was torn from top to bottom. It did not wear out, nor was it an accident or an act of vandalism by men. God himself tore it — from top to bottom.

The torn curtain meant accomplishment

On the cross Jesus said, 'It is finished.' He was not referring to his life being ended, but, rather, to God's plan of salvation being completed. We have seen that God's way of saving sinners was no last-minute thought, but a meticulously planned way to which the Old Testament Scriptures pointed. Now this plan was finished; it was accomplished. The tearing of the curtain proclaimed the end of the old covenant and the beginning of the new.

The tearing of the curtain was a sign that the Old Testament sacrificial system was no longer needed. Its work of pointing to the Christ was done. There was no longer any need for priest, sacrifices and altars. Jesus the true High Priest had appeared. Jesus the Lamb of God was the last sacrifice that God accepted, and the cross was the last altar needed. To maintain a priesthood and altar now is to deny the accomplishment of Calvary.

Hebrews 7:24-25 tells us that 'Because Jesus lives for ever, he has a permanent priesthood. Therefore he is able to save completely those who come to God through him.' Two reasons are then given for Christ's unique ministry as our priest and sacrifice: First, 'Because he always lives to intercede for them' (v. 25) and, second, 'He sacrificed for their sins once for all when he offered himself' (v. 27).

At Calvary something glorious and wondrous has been accomplished, and the torn curtain proclaims it. Everything now is different. In the words of Horatius Bonar's hymn:

> No blood, no altar now: the sacrifice is o'er;
> No flame, no smoke ascends on high,
> The Lamb is slain no more.
> But richer blood has flowed from nobler veins,
> To purge the soul from guilt
> And cleanse the reddest stains.
>
> We thank thee for the blood;
> The blood of Christ, thy Son;

The blood by which our peace is made,
The victory is won;
Great victory o'er hell and sin and woe,
That needs no second fight
And leaves no second foe.

The torn curtain meant access

The curtain separated men from God. It pronounced that no one was worthy to come into God's presence. The only exception was the High Priest as the people's representative. This concession of divine grace only served to further underline that sinners were not welcome. The people all knew this. They knew that the Most Holy Place was barred to them, and so the reality of God's presence was far removed. But with the finished work of Jesus, now we read this: 'Therefore, brothers, since we have confidence to enter the Most Holy Place by the blood of Jesus, by a new and living way opened for us through the curtain, that is, his body, and since we have a great priest over the house of God, let us draw near to God with a sincere heart in full assurance of faith' (Heb. 10:19-22).

We can now draw near to God because God himself has removed the barrier. The Most Holy Place and the mercy seat are opened to all sinners who trust in Jesus as God's only way of salvation. There is now no 'keep out' curtain, but rather the gospel invitation to draw near. Access to God has been bought for us by the death of Jesus.

The curtain symbolized what really keeps us from God, which is our sin: 'Your iniquities have separated you from your God; your sins have hidden his face from you, so that he will not hear' (Isa. 59:2). But on the cross Jesus dealt with our sin, and, as a result, 'Now in Christ Jesus you who once were far away have been brought near through the blood of Christ' (Eph. 2:13).

This is God's way of salvation.

The torn curtain meant acceptance

The curtain said, 'Keep out, you have no place here because you are not acceptable to God.' The tearing of that curtain proclaims a different message: 'When Christ came as high priest of the good things that are already here, he went through the greater and more perfect tabernacle that is not man-made, that is to say, not a part of this creation. He did not enter by means of the blood of goats and calves; but he entered the Most Holy Place once for all by his own blood, having obtained eternal redemption' (Heb. 9:11-12).

Jesus has obtained eternal redemption for us. In other words, he has made the guilty sinner acceptable to God by covering our sin and paying our debt. In the Lord Jesus Christ — and in him alone — we are acceptable to God. The Lord has opened up a way for us to come to him.

God's immediate confirmation that he accepts Christ's death in the place of guilty sinners is the tearing of the curtain. The great and glorious confirmation of the res-

urrection had to wait for another three days, but immediately Jesus died, the curtain was torn.

The way to God is open and God's invitation to sinners is to draw near.

IV. The cross for us today

13. The message of the cross

The gospel has always been a difficult message for people to believe and accept. The difficulty lies not in the gospel itself, but in men and women. Some may feel that such a statement is a cop-out made by Christians to explain the fact that most people reject the gospel. But this is not so. The gospel is unattractive and unappealing to people. They don't want it. This is not something new; Paul had the same trouble at Corinth in the first century. In the first chapter of 1 Corinthians, the apostle grapples with people's negative response to the gospel (vv. 18-25).

The message of the cross literally means the 'word' of the cross. It's the Greek word *logos*. The same word is used in John 1:1: 'In the beginning was the *Word*, and the *Word* was with God and the *Word* was God.' It means all that the cross represents and stands for — it means the doctrine of the cross.

The biblical teaching about the cross started long before Jesus was born. Understanding the Old Testament messianic prophecies — for example, in the Psalms, Isaiah and Zechariah — is crucial if we are to grasp fully the meaning of the cross. Those prophecies point clearly to Jesus and are amazing in their accuracy.

When we come to the New Testament and the life of
Jesus, we find him saying, time and time again, that he
was going to be put to death. He wasn't speaking in a
mood of pessimistic fatalism, but because he knew that
this was why he came into the world. Drawing on the
Old Testament, Jesus likened himself to the snake in the
desert: 'Just as Moses lifted up the snake in the desert, so
the Son of Man must be lifted up, that every one who
believes in him may have eternal life' (John 3:14-15). By
'lifted up,' Jesus was describing his death on the cross
(John 12:32-33).

Throughout the New Testament, the message of the
cross is clear. Peter said, 'He himself bore our sins in his
body on the tree' (1 Peter 2:24). John said, 'The blood
of Jesus, his Son, purifies us from every sin' (1 John 1:7).
In 1 Corinthians 1:23, Paul stresses, 'We preach Christ
crucified', and at the beginning of the next chapter (v. 2),
he makes the point that he resolved or determined to
preach nothing else to the Corinthians but 'Christ and
him crucified'. Why did the apostle feel and act this way?
It was because of the cross. If you are a Christian, the
message of the cross is that Jesus took your sin, guilt and
punishment. He faced the wrath and judgement of God
instead of you and died in your place, and so God is
now able to justly forgive you for all your sin.

No wonder the gospel is 'good news'! Could there ever
be better news? That instead of spending an eternity in
hell, we can be accepted in heaven? By any reasonable
standard, you would expect that people would be
delighted with that.

If there was a particular job about the house that
needed to be done that I dreaded facing and kept putting

off, I would be overjoyed if I got home and found that a neighbour had done the job for me. My gratitude would be enormous. I would rush to his home to thank my kind friend. That would be a normal reaction. So why don't people gladly receive the message of the cross?

'Foolishness'

Paul says, 'The message of the cross is foolishness to those who are perishing' (1 Cor. 1:18). This really is incredible. Here are people who are *perishing*. In Scripture, that means far more than death; it means that they are plunging into hell, for ever to experience divine wrath. Yet these people, when they hear of God's guaranteed remedy to this, dismiss it as foolishness. Why do they act in this way? Paul answers this in the following verses. 'Jews demand miraculous signs and Greeks look for wisdom, but we preach Christ crucified; a stumbling block to Jews and foolishness to Gentiles' (1 Cor. 1:22-23).

The cross is God's only way of dealing in love and mercy with human sin. Jesus bore our sin, said Peter (1 Peter 2:24). God laid our sin upon Jesus, said Isaiah (Isa. 53:6). God made Jesus to be sin for us, said Paul (2 Cor. 5:21). All these verses speak of Jesus becoming the sinner's substitute and dying instead of us. This is portrayed perfectly in the Old Testament scapegoat (Lev. 16:8-11). The scapegoat on the Day of Atonement was the innocent victim taking away the sin of the guilty.

The Jews wanted proof. 'Show us! Prove it!', they were continually saying. Their preconceived notion of the Messiah as a great political and military leader made them reject Christ. A crucified Messiah was to them a contradiction in terms. Thus the cross was to them a stumbling block.

The Greeks prided themselves in their superior wisdom and philosophical thought. They felt they were intellectually superior to everyone else. The cross was foolishness to them — it was outrageous and absurd. The response of these first-century rejecters of the gospel is exactly the same as that of most folk today — preconceived ideas about themselves and God, and speculative thought about how God should and would act.

Modern thinking

The message of the cross speaks of human sin and guilt, of divine wrath and judgement. Today, people reject both sin and judgement, so they change the message of the cross. They sentimentalize it or shroud it in superstition so that the cross becomes nothing more than a lucky charm. Basically, people reject the cross as God's answer to human sin because they do not see sin as a problem. Therefore, there's no need for an answer. But the fact is that men and women are perishing and going to hell.

In the Bible, God warns us over and over again of the terrible consequence of sin. The message of the cross comes to us with its invitation of salvation, but also with its warning if we reject the message — and yet still men reject it; they do not take their sin seriously.

During the first Gulf War, Iraq launched Scud missiles against Israel. These were terrible weapons that gave only one minute's warning of approaching destruction and death. When that warning came, the Israelis fled to shelters for protection. Everyone ran for cover because they knew the danger was real. It would have been stupid to reject the warning and refuse the shelter.

The Christian is someone who has seen that he faces a far greater danger than that threatened by Scud missiles: he has seen his sin and takes it seriously. He has heeded God's warning and has fled to Christ for shelter, forgiveness and salvation.

The power of God

The opposite of foolishness is wisdom, and therefore we would expect Paul in 1 Corinthians 1:18 to go on to say that for the Christian the message of the cross is wisdom. This he does later in the chapter, but not in verse 18. In verse 18, he says that, to those who are saved, the gospel is the power of God. The gospel is not just some good advice telling us how we ought to behave. It's not even news about God's power — it *is* God's power.

In 1991, the Americans came up with an answer to the Scud missile —the Patriot missile that could knock those terrible messengers of death out of the sky. This wasn't an infallible answer, for some Scuds got through. But God's answer to the terrible power of sin is infallible. In the cross, God did something that took tremendous power: he saved sinners. He destroyed the power of sin and Satan, and he now gives to his people the new life of the resurrected Christ. The cross demonstrates divine power as well as divine love.

When you consider Calvary and the power that God exercised to save souls, it's amazing that people can think that good deeds, or a few prayers, or baptism, or church attendance, or giving to charity can ever save their souls.

Christians are not saved because they have all their questions and doubts answered. They didn't come to Christ in faith because their intellect was satisfied. While it's true that God never bypasses the sinner's mind in order to speak to the heart, the sinner is only saved because he or she is deeply convicted that he or she needs saving, and that Jesus is the only Saviour. The power of God in the gospel both convicts and saves. The Christian looks at the cross and cries with delight, 'That's how God saved me!'

14. Christ lifted up

When Jesus entered Jerusalem in triumph on Palm Sunday, the prophecy of Zechariah chapter nine was fulfilled. Calvary was only five days away. In John 12:27, Jesus said, 'Now my heart is troubled.' The prospect of the cross and all that it involved was proving daunting to the Saviour, but he had no intention of avoiding it. He didn't ask his Father to save him from the cross, because the cross was the sole reason he came into the world. He came to die for his people, to give his life a ransom for us, and the cross was the God-ordained way that this was to be done.

In John 12:32, Jesus talks about being lifted up. John in the next verse adds an explanation of what the Saviour meant. He was, says John, referring to the kind of death he was going to die. The kind of death Jesus was going to experience, or the way he was going to die, was most important. The way he died must clearly demonstrate who he was and what he was doing. Crucifixion was the only kind of death that could do both these things. Stoning to death, the normal Jewish way of execution, would not.

Crucifixion showed who Jesus was because it fulfilled the Old Testament prophecies about the Messiah. Psalm 22, that great messianic passage, not only foresaw Jesus forsaken by his Father (v. 1), the reaction of the crowd (v. 7), and the behaviour of the soldiers (v. 18), but it also gives a remarkable description of the physical agonies of crucifixion: 'I am poured out like water, and all my bones are out of joint. My heart has turned to wax; it has melted away within me. My strength is dried up like a potsherd, and my tongue sticks to the roof of my mouth; you lay me in the dust of death. Dogs have surrounded me; a band of evil men has encircled me, they have pierced my hands and my feet. I can count all my bones; people stare and gloat over me' (vv. 14-17).

The Phoenicians were the first to devise crucifixion. They considered that all other means of execution were too quick. With crucifixion, men could die very slowly; death on a cross could take two or three days. The Jews never used crucifixion, but the Romans did, and they developed it to an exact science with a set of rules to be followed.

Crucifixion showed what Jesus was doing. In Galatians 3:13, Paul said that when Jesus was hung on the tree (i.e., the cross), he 'redeemed us from the curse of the law by becoming a curse for us'. Such a statement should cause every believer to gasp in wonder before the cross. The curse of the law is its penal judgement upon sin and, therefore, Jesus faced that instead of us.

The Saviour goes on in John 12 to mention three things that his death would accomplish:

First, his death would accomplish the judgement of the world (v. 31). 'Now,' said Jesus, meaning not at the exact moment he was speaking, but in the whole proceedings of his death. The cross is the judgement of the world because, in rejecting Jesus so viciously, the world was rejecting its only hope of salvation. To reject Jesus was to reject God.

At the same time he was uttering these words, Jesus told the parable of the tenants: 'Therefore, when the owner of the vineyard comes, what will he do to those tenants? He will bring those wretches to a wretched end, they replied, and he will rent the vineyard to other tenants, who will give him his share of the crop at harvest time' (Matt. 21:40-41). To reject the Son of God leaves men with nothing but the unending wrath and judgement of God.

The same truth was taught by Jesus in John 3 when he refers to the Old Testament incident of Moses and the snake in the desert. Sin brings judgement, and 'The Lord sent venomous snakes among them; they bit the people and many Israelites died' (Num. 21:6). The only answer to this judgement of God was God's own answer, which was for the people to look to the bronze snake lifted up on a pole in the midst of them. Jesus said that this is a perfect example of what the cross means, but if men refuse to look to the cross as the provision of God's love and mercy for sinners, they will be left with their sin and its consequence.

Second, Jesus' death will drive out the 'prince of this world' (v. 31). The 'prince of this world' is a phrase that only Jesus used, and he did so three times to refer to Satan (John 12:31; 14:30; 16:11). Satan is the 'prince of this world' because he reigns in the hearts of men and women. Jesus acknowledges this by using the title. But men and women are God's creation, made in God's image. Satan's reign is due to sin. Sin and death are his weapons and they seem to be invincible.

D. A. Carson writes, 'Although the cross might seem like Satan's triumph, it is in fact his defeat. In one sense Satan was defeated by the out-breaking power of the kingdom of God even within the ministry of Jesus (Luke 10:18). But the fundamental smashing of his reign of tyranny takes place in the death and exaltation of Jesus. When Jesus was glorified, lifted up to heaven by means of the cross, enthroned, then too was Satan dethroned. What residual power God permits the prince of this world to enjoy is further curtailed by the Holy Spirit, the Counsellor (John 16:11).'[1]

Third, the death of Jesus will draw all men to himself (v. 32). The lifting up of Jesus on the cross wasn't only the physical act of lifting his body on a piece of wood, but also involved the means of exalting and enthroning him on his return to the Father in heaven. From his exalted position at the right hand of the Father, Jesus uses what was accomplished on the cross to draw men and women to himself.

When Jesus said 'all men,' he did not mean everyone without exception. He's not putting forward the teaching of universal salvation (or universal atonement), because that would be to deny his many clear teachings that all will *not* be saved. 'All men' means all *types* of people — men and women from all nations, like the Greeks of verse 20, whose coming to Jesus prompted the whole discourse in John 12 about his death. The cross is the great proof of God's determined actions to pardon sin. When Jesus died, it was to bring to God not sinners condemned by their sin, but sinners pardoned by what Jesus did for them at Calvary. This drawing of sinners to Christ is accomplished by the preaching of the message

of the cross. As sinners hear the message and are convicted by the Holy Spirit both of their sin and of the hope
of salvation, so Jesus draws them to himself. He draws
them with great tenderness and love. He draws them
gently with the assurance that they will be received.

Jesus said, 'No one can come to me unless the Father
who sent me draws him' (John 6:44), but — praise
God — he also said, 'All that the Father gives me will
come to me, and whoever comes to me I will never drive
away' (John 6:37).

15. The triumph of the cross

On the cross, Jesus dealt with two things that opposed man and doomed him to spiritual bondage and eternal damnation. These two things are shown to us by Paul in Colossians chapter two: the *law* — 'having cancelled the written code, with its regulations, that was against us and that stood opposed to us; he [Jesus] took it away, nailing it to the cross' (v. 14) — and the *powers of darkness* — 'And having disarmed the powers and authorities, he [Jesus] made a public spectacle of them, triumphing over them by the cross' (v. 15).

As we enter the twenty-first century, we hear a great deal about demons and exorcism. They are openly portrayed in books and films. Some folk are terrified by all this, while others treat it as a means of entertainment. Many do not take it seriously and regard horoscopes, tarot cards and Ouija boards as harmless fun. Some are puzzled by the phenomena. Others reject it as medieval nonsense.

But to anyone who reads the Bible, this is not new or strange. Christ and his apostles often cast out devils. Mary Magdalene was said to have been possessed by seven devils. Moreover, the Bible teaches that all men

and women, outside of Christ, are dominated and
controlled by the devil (Eph. 2:1-3).

Probably only a handful of people deliberately set out
to worship Satan, but there are millions who ignore God;
therefore, whether they acknowledge it or not, they are
also living according to Satan's dictates. There are also
many who believe they are Christians, but they have
never repented of their sin, never been born again. It's of
this type of person that Jesus said in John 8:44, 'You
belong to your father, the devil, and you want to carry
out your father's desire.' John's conclusion is that 'The
whole world is under the control of the evil one'
(1 John 5:19).

All Christians were once in this condition. That's why
Jesus came to save us. The law of God is against us, not
because it is wrong, but because *we* are wrong. This
gives Satan the power to enslave us and to accuse us
before God. Satan wields the law of God to accuse and
condemn us. Jesus came to change this by satisfying the
law and paying the debt our sin had incurred, so break-
ing Satan's power.

Satan

The reference in Colossians 2:15 to 'powers and authorities' is to all unseen spiritual beings (as in 1:16 and
2:10). But the verse also refers specifically to Satan and
his fallen angels — the powers of darkness as in Ephesians 6:12: 'For our struggle is not against flesh and
blood, but against the rulers, against the authorities,

against the powers of this dark world and against the
spiritual forces of evil in the heavenly realms.'

The Bible has no doubt as to the actual personality of
Satan. Many people treat him as a joke, a comical figure
dressed up in red tights with horns and a tail. It's notice-
able in recent years how often ads on TV have utilized
this comical figure to sell their goods. But Satan is no
joke; neither is he an abstract power of evil.

There's never any question in Scripture but that Satan
is a real person. It's important that we understand and
believe this. Dr Martyn Lloyd-Jones wrote, 'A belief in
the devil and his powers is an absolute essential to a
belief in the biblical teaching concerning sin and evil.
You cannot really believe the biblical doctrine concerning
sin unless you believe in the devil and in the principalities and powers associated with him. Further, a belief in
the devil and his forces is absolutely essential to a true
understanding of the biblical doctrine of salvation. "Ah,
but," you say, "that cannot be. Surely, all that is necessary is that I believe Christ died for my sins upon the
cross." So far you are right, but why did he have to
come? What was he really doing on the cross? According
to the apostle Paul, he was there, "spoiling principalities
and powers, making a show of them openly, and triumphing over them in it" (Col. 2:15, AV). Why did
Christ have to come? One of his own answers was this:
"The strong man armed keepeth his goods at peace, but
when a stronger than he cometh upon him, he taketh
from him all his armour in which he trusted, and divideth
his spoils" (Luke 11:21-22, AV). Do not think that you
can understand the biblical doctrine of salvation and
reject the devil. You cannot! You do not hold the true

doctrine of salvation if you do not believe in the devil and his powers.'[1]

Jesus versus Satan

On the cross Jesus dealt with the law and bore the wrath of a sin-hating God for us, but he also dealt with Satan and his all-consuming grip on souls. At Calvary the most terrible battle of history took place. Jesus said on the night before the cross, 'The prince of this world [the devil] is coming against me' (John 14:30). In this battle our souls were at stake as the satanic powers bombarded Jesus. In the darkness of midday and in the body and nature of man, Jesus battled for our eternal souls. The battle started at Bethlehem when Satan moved his puppet, King Herod, to try to kill the baby Jesus. It continued for the next thirty-three years, as the temptation in the wilderness shows us, but it reached its climax at Calvary.

Charles Spurgeon has an amazing passage in a sermon on Colossians 2:15. He said, 'But the cross was the centre of the battle; there, on the top of Calvary, must the dread fight of eternity be fought. Now must the Son of God arise, and gird his sword upon his thigh. Dread defeat or glorious conquest awaits the champion of the church. Which shall it be? We hold our breath with anxious suspense while the storm is raging. I hear the trumpet sound. The howlings and yells of hell rise in awful clamour. The pit is emptying out its legions. Terrible as lions, hungry as wolves, and black as night, the demons rush on in myriads. Satan's reserve-forces — those who

had long been kept against this day of terrible battle —
are roaring from their dens. See how countless are their
armies, and how fierce their countenances. Brandishing
his sword, the archfiend leads the van, bidding his fol-
lowers fight neither with small or great, save only with
the King of Israel. Terrible are the leaders of the battle.
Sin is there, with all its innumerable offspring, spitting
forth the venom of asps, and infixing their poison fangs
in the Saviour's flesh. Death is there upon his pale horse,
and his cruel dart rends its way through the body of
Jesus even to his inward heart. One man — nay, tell it,
lest any should misunderstand me — one God stands in
battle array against ten thousands of principalities and
powers. On, on they come, and he receives them all.'[2]

Triumph

The language of Colossians 2:15 is taken from a triumph
of the Roman army. A victorious general would parade
in triumph through Rome with the captured kings and
generals chained to his chariot. In this way Paul depicts
Christ's triumph over Satan: the evil one is defeated and
chained to the chariot of our Saviour. On the cross, Jesus
disarmed Satan and took away his power. Spurgeon in
that remarkable sermon describes this disarming: 'Satan
came against Christ; he had in his hand a sharp sword
called the law, dipped in the poison of sin, so that every
wound which the law inflicted was deadly. Christ dashed
this sword out of Satan's hand, and there stood the
prince of darkness unarmed. His helmet was cleft in
twain, and his head was crushed as with a rod of iron.

Death rose against Christ. The Saviour snatched his quiver from him, emptied out all his darts, cut them in two, gave Death back the feather end, but kept the poisoned barbs from him, that he might never destroy the ransomed. Sin came against Christ; but Sin was utterly cut in pieces. It had been Satan's armour bearer, but its shield was cast away, and it lay dead upon the plain. Is it not a noble picture to behold all the enemies of Christ — nay, my brethren, all your enemies, and mine — totally disarmed? Satan has nothing left him now wherewith he may attack us. He may attempt to injure us, but wound us he never can, for his sword and spear are utterly taken away.'[3]

As we saw in Zechariah 3, Satan is silenced by our new garment of righteousness. He can no longer accuse us because the law is satisfied in Jesus, fully paying our debt. What a glorious triumph this is! On the cross, Jesus made a public spectacle of his victory. The whole world was witness to it, and still is every time a sinner is saved. The triumph of the cross was complete. Jesus had anticipated this on Palm Sunday when he said, 'Now is the time for the judgement of this world; now the prince of this world will be driven out' (John 12:31).

The relationship between verses 14 and 15 of Colossians 2 is important. Man because of his sinful nature violates God's law. So the law, instead of being a blessing to us, becomes a curse. Therefore, Satan can quite properly use it to accuse and condemn us. We are guilty — 'The power of sin is the law' (1 Cor. 15:56). But on the cross, Jesus fulfils the righteousness of the law for us. He pays our debt and takes the cancelled statement of debt, nailing it to the cross as proof of payment.

When we are saved, the triumph of the cross becomes our triumph. Satan can still tempt us, but he can no longer compel us. His influence is still strong in the world, but it's limited in the lives of God's people. He is chained like the lions in *The Pilgrim's Progress.* As Christians, we should live in the reality of the triumph of the cross. We are no longer slaves to sin; so, therefore, we are not to let sin reign in our lives (Rom. 6:6, 12).

16. Grace

The fact that Jesus loved me could not in and of itself save me. Thank God that Paul is able to go on and say, 'and gave himself for me'. Here is love leading to grace and mercy; love issuing in a great act of sacrifice.

In Ephesians 2:4-5, three great gospel words are used: 'But because of his great *love* for us, God, who is rich in *mercy*, made us alive with Christ even when we were dead in transgressions — it is by *grace* you have been saved.' Love, mercy and grace all speak of something God does. Out of God's *love* flow mercy and grace. *Mercy* is God not giving us what we deserve, and *grace* is God giving us what we do not deserve. Because of our sin, we deserve punishment, but instead God gives us pardon. The last thing we deserve is salvation, but in grace God saves us.

Grace is not some vague notion but, rather, a definite act on the part of God. It is God doing for the sinner what no one else could do and what the sinner could never accomplish for him or herself. It is the love of God that makes Calvary possible, but it is the holiness of God that makes it necessary. Grace flows out of divine love and fully satisfies God's holiness. When grace begins its work it never forgets the absolute holiness of God. Therefore it has to provide for the sinner a salvation that does not gloss over or minimize the effect of sin. There must be no short-cut salvation, no salvation on the cheap, no theoretical dealing with sin. God's holiness cannot be deceived or satisfied with such things. The objective of grace is not merely to make sinners accept God, but to make it possible for the holy God to accept sinners.

How does grace do this?

The riches of God's grace provide a sacrifice of immense value for sin. It is the quality of the sacrifice that satisfies God's holiness: 'In him we have redemption through his blood, the forgiveness of sins, in accordance with the riches of God's grace' (Eph. 1:7). 'But now in Christ Jesus you who once were far away have been brought near through the blood of Christ' (Eph. 2:13).

The sacrifice is Christ, and the key word in both the above verses is 'blood'. The riches of grace are seen in the infinite value of the sacrifice it provides. God gave his best for sinners. God gave his Son to atone for our rebellion. God did this because only the blood of Christ could fully pay the debt that human sin had incurred.

God's holiness demanded that sin should be dealt with justly and legally. That meant that it must be punished, and the punishment required was death, separation from God. There could be no salvation without this require-ment being fully met. God's grace provides the answer in making Jesus responsible for our sin. God lays that sin upon Jesus; with the sin goes the guilt, and with the guilt goes the punishment.

The word 'blood' means the sacrificial, atoning death of Jesus on the cross when he died as our substitute. It is grace alone that gives the sinner hope; because salvation is by the free grace of God in Christ, there is hope for us all. Grace is for sinners and we are all sinners. This is the hope of the gospel and God's way of salvation.

How do we benefit from grace?

The answer to this crucial question is also found in Ephesians 2: 'For it is by grace you have been saved, through faith — and this not from yourselves, it is the gift of God — not by works, so that no one can boast' (vv. 8-9). Grace comes to us through faith. Faith is the channel by which the saving grace of God comes to sinners. It is a gift given to us so that we are wonderfully able to repent from our sins, believe in the Lord Jesus and be saved. Faith is not some false optimism or misplaced self-confidence. Neither is it something vague or indefinite. It looks towards what God has done for us in the Lord Jesus Christ. It is not a step into the dark but a step out of the dark into the light. It responds to the light of gospel truth that God brings to our hearts and minds.

Faith throws itself upon the mercy and grace of God. The only reason for the existence of faith is grace. What God has done is the only thing worth putting your faith in. Faith trusts that what Jesus did in dying for sinners is enough to satisfy the holiness of God and the demands of divine law. Faith is believing God and calling upon Jesus for forgiveness and salvation.

True faith

There are many imitations of faith but true faith always has two essential qualities.

First, it trusts only in Jesus. It is not Jesus plus my own efforts or plus anything else. Faith gets to the heart of the issue, which is: What does the sinner need to be acceptable to God? Jesus as our Saviour is all we need; therefore faith rests in Jesus alone.

Secondly, faith motivates a response to God's gracious invitation in the gospel. It brings us to Christ in repentance and enables us to receive the free gift of salvation. We read in Acts 11:21 that 'A great number of people believed and turned to the Lord.' The evidence that their faith was real was that they acted upon what they believed and turned to the Lord for the grace of salvation.

God has graciously invited you to come to him for salvation. He has given strength to his invitation by sending Jesus to pay the price of your sins. The grace of God has provided all the means for you to be saved. The new birth and faith are gifts that God gives us, and he expects us then to believe and to come to him in repentance. Faith is an activity of the sinner, not God. In faith we trust in all that God has done for us in the Lord Jesus Christ.

Notes

Chapter 3
[1] David Baron, *Commentary on Zechariah: his visions and prophecies* (Grand Rapids: Kregel Publications).

[2] C. F. Keil, *The twelve minor prophets*, volume 2 (Grand Rapids: Wm. B. Eerdmans Publishing Co., 1965), p.397.

Chapter 8
[1] C. H. Spurgeon, *The gospel of the kingdom* (London: Passmore and Alabaster, 1893), p.27.

[2] Hugh Martin, *The shadow of Calvary* (Edinburgh: Banner of Truth Trust, 1983), pp.32-33.

[3] As above.

[4] Louis Berkhof, *Systematic theology* (Grand Rapids: Wm. B. Eerdmans Publishing Co., 1988), p.318.

[5] Robert Traill in David Brown, *The four Gospels* (Edinburgh: Banner of Truth Trust, 1998), p.332.

[6] D. A. Carson, *The Gospel according to John* (Grand Rapids: Wm. B. Eerdmans Publishing Co., 1991), pp.576-77.

[7] As above.

Chapter 9
[1] J. C. Ryle.

[2] Martin, *The shadow of Calvary*.

Chapter 10
[1] Martin, *The shadow of Calvary*.

[2] Leon Morris, *The cross in the New Testament* (Grand Rapids: Wm. B. Eerdmans Publishing Co., 1965).

[3] As above.

Chapter 14
[1] Carson, *The Gospel according to John.*

Chapter 15
[1] D. Martyn Lloyd-Jones.

[2] C. H. Spurgeon, *New Park Street Pulpit,* (London: Passmore and Alabaster, 1859), pp.386-88.

[3] As above.

A wide range of Christian books is available from Evangelical Press. If you would like a free catalogue please write to us or contact us by e-mail. Alternatively, you can view the whole catalogue online at our website:

www.evangelicalpress.org.

Evangelical Press
Faverdale North, Darlington, Co. Durham, DL3 0PH, England

e-mail: sales@evangelicalpress.org

Evangelical Press USA
P. O. Box 825, Webster, New York 14580, USA

e-mail: usa.sales@evangelicalpress.org